The
JOY of
Being
Single

The Joy of Being Single

By Allia Zobel

Illustrated by Roz Chast

Enjoy!

Workman Publishing, New York

Library of Congress Cataloging-in-Publication Data

Zobel, Allia

The joy of being single / by Allia Zobel : illustrated by Roz Chast.
p.   cm.
ISBN 1-56305-124-9 (pbk.) : $5.95
1. Single women—Humor.   2. Single women—Caricatures and cartoons.
I. Chast, Roz.   II. Title.
PN6231.S5485Z63   1992
741.5'973—dc20   91-50959
CIP

Books are available at special discounts when purchased in bulk for premiums
and sales promotions as well as for fund-raising or educational use. Special editions
or book excerpts can also be created to specification. For details, contact the
Special Sales Director at the address below.

Workman Publishing
708 Broadway
New York, New York 10003
Manufactured in United States of America
First printing May 1992
3   5   7   9   10   8   6   4

For my parents, Alvin and Lucille,
my departed friend Judith, my cat Scruffy, and
all the men who never married me.

*Being single's gotten a bad rap. It's not awful. It's always interesting. And from my point of view, it has great benefits.
A friend of mine who's getting married doesn't agree. She bet me her little black book I couldn't come up with twenty good reasons.*

I sure hope those guys like to cook.

—A.Z.

You don't have to be nice to anybody's mother but your own.

You can vacuum whenever you want—or not at all.

You don't have to make up excuses if you dent your car.

You never have to watch *Monday Night Football*.

You can cut your toenails in bed.

You can bring home Sara Lee cake for two and eat both portions.

You can rip out anything you want from the newspaper.

You can use all the hot water. And you never have to worry about taking the last clean towel, which you can leave in a wet clump by the tub when you're through with it.

You can hang wet pantyhose or just-cleaned car mats over the shower rod.

You can take a two-hour soak. And there's no problem if you forget to clean the tub.

Best of all, there's never a wait for the bathroom.

You can use all the hot water.

You can put cream on your face, petroleum jelly
and gloves on your hands, and wear an old
T-shirt to bed.

You never have to tell anyone how your day was.

You can
go dancing
until 3 A.M.,
no questions
asked.

You can eat cold pizza for breakfast, jelly beans and a Coke for dinner.

Hideous

Ghastly

Disgusting

Not very attractive

Peculiar

Icky

Deranged

No one will laugh when you say you have nothing to wear.

You can sit in a chair and read a novel cover to cover without feeling guilty.

You can drink the last cold beer.

No one will mind if you take a course in
Mideast lentils.

You won't annoy anyone if you whistle birdcalls while you paint your nails.

Sleeping is always bliss. You can snore all you want, hog the sheets, and take your cat or your dog to bed if you want to.

You can turn on the air-conditioner for white noise—even if it's winter—and leave on all the lights when you get up in the middle of the night.

Then, too, you won't offend anyone if you just fall asleep on the couch after dinner, either.

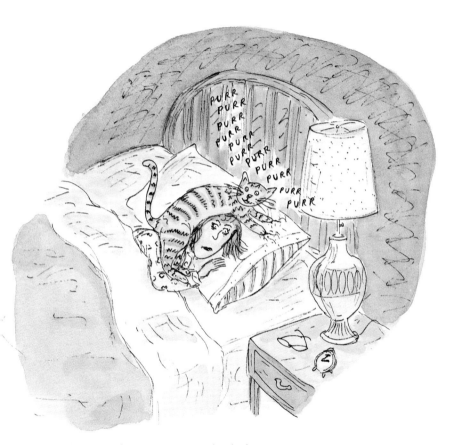

You can take your cat to bed if you want to.

The money you save on anniversary gifts can be spent on sending your laundry out.

If you get only one ticket to a Billy Joel concert, you can go without feeling guilty.

You can spend $150 on a haircut without fear of reprisals.

You'll never have to change and/or hyphenate your name—unless, of course, you want to.

You know
when you're
out of milk.

You can play the same record over and over again.

You can keep everything
where it's easiest for you
to reach it, use it,
pet it, eat it,
look at it
and store it.

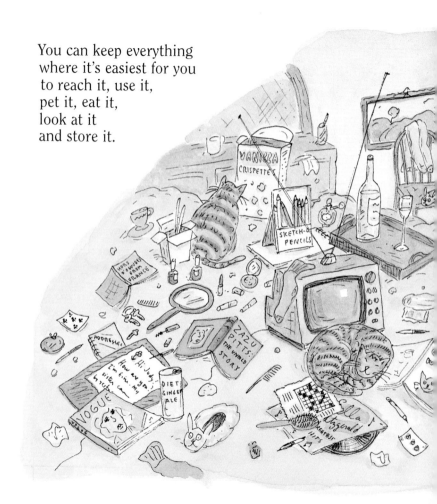

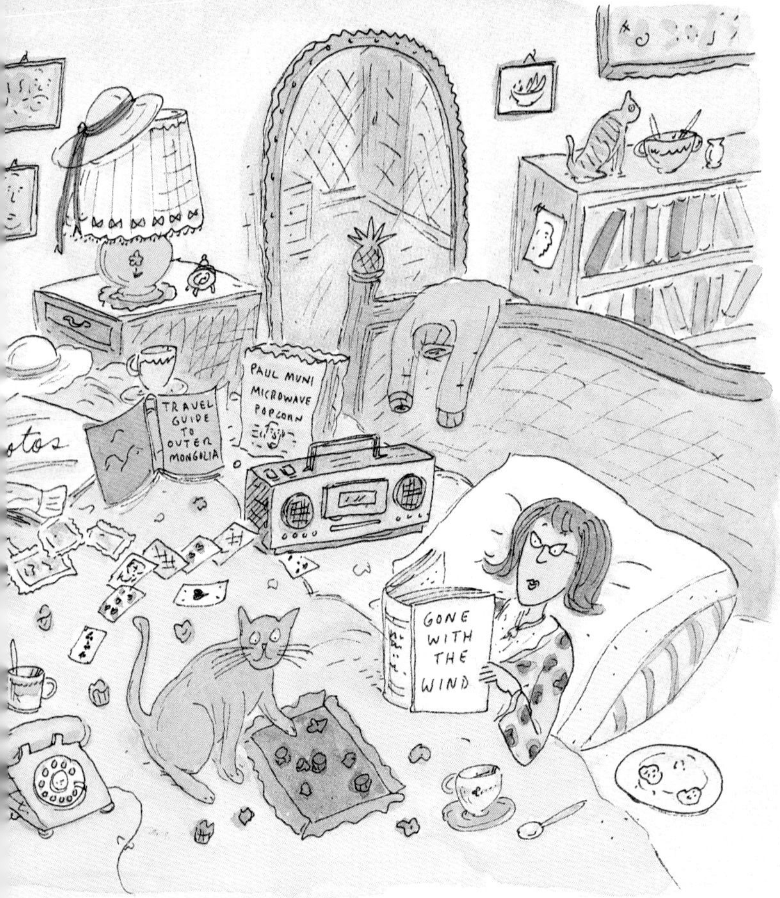

otos
TRAVEL GUIDE TO OUTER MONGOLIA
PAUL MUNI MICROWAVE POPCORN
GONE WITH THE WIND

You never have to pick out bridesmaids' dresses.

When you get a box of candy, you can stick your fingers in all the pieces to see which one is best.

You can make as much noise as you want when you eat.

You don't have to worry about anyone drinking your contact lenses when you leave them in a glass overnight.

Dirty dishes. You can wash them immediately or leave them in the oven. You can pile them on the counter for days, or weeks, or until you run out.

If you scorch a pot and can't get it clean, you can just toss it, no questions asked.

Then again, you can just eat off paper plates and be done with it.

You can pile them on the counter for days, or
weeks, or until you run out.

It doesn't matter how you open the cereal box.

You can have a video marathon on Saturday instead of cleaning.

You don't have to worry about earning more money
than anyone else.

You can wear as much makeup as you want.

FILOGUYS. APRIL

16 MON Ed, Mike, Tod, Lars, Claude, Tim, Jim, Steve, Rick, Little Ed, Nilo, Mark, Jeff, Tom, Garth

17 TUES Nick, Joey, Lucky, Everett, Wally, Phil, Bob, Sandro, Potter, Mick, Thomas, Kevin, Evan, Ross

18 WED Andrew, Matthew, Ivan, Tucker, William, Judd, Spencer, Wheeler, George, Norman

19 THURS Connor, Mitch, Lon, Dwayne, Harvey, Otis, Kyle, Sean, Paul, Grant, Ellery, Dino, Allan

20 FRI Walker, Niles, Gregory, Chuckie, Samuel, Aaron, Sal, Vernon, Quincy, Waldo, Jacob

21 SAT Loddie, Peter, Kelly, Carter, Jules, David, Topper, Al, Kurt, Rodney, Rufus, Whitey, Gus

22 SUN Barney, Barry, Wayne, Buzz, John, Jack, Nathan, Benjamin, Alexander, Aloysious, Warren

You
can date
as many
people
as you
can keep
track of.

You never have to fight about turning down the electric blanket.

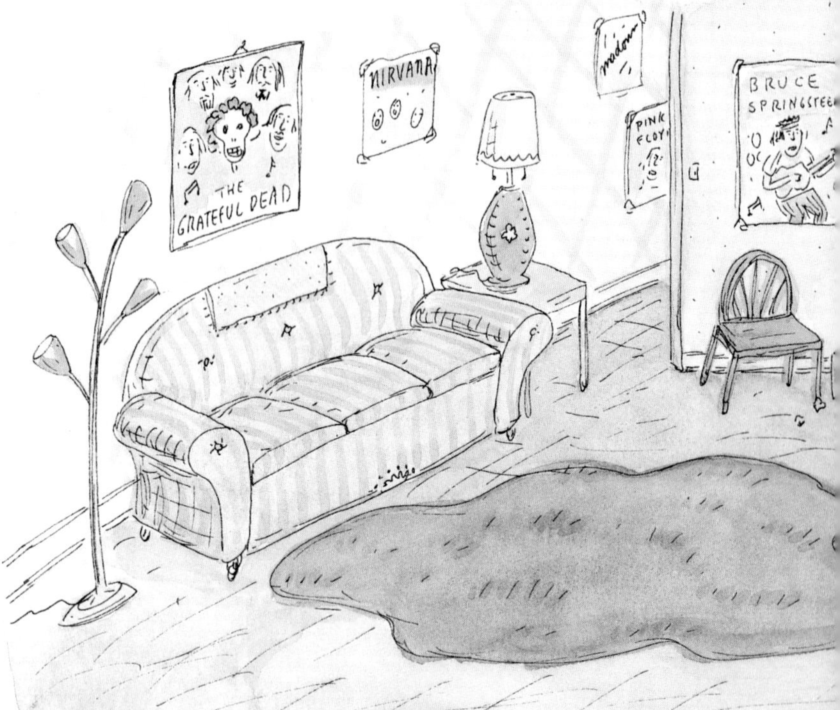
THE GRATEFUL DEAD
NIRVANA
BRUCE

You can decorate your apartment with posters of The Grateful Dead, or paint the kitchen purple and pink, without anyone making a fuss.

If you win the lottery, you don't have to share it.

You don't need a sensible reason to buy a new dress.

You can go to the museum and spend all day
staring at the Picassos.

You can talk to yourself as much as you want.

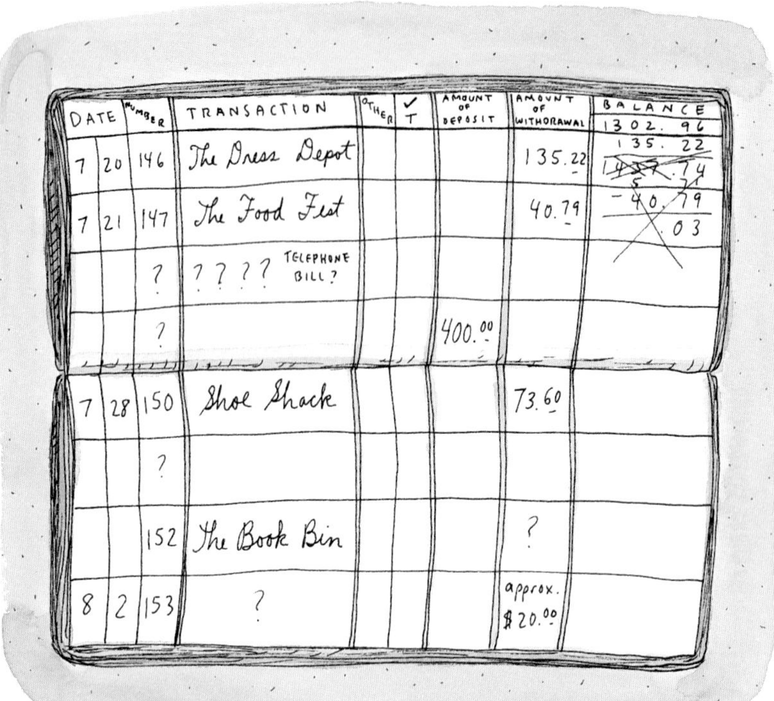

DATE	NUMBER	TRANSACTION	OTHER	✓ T	AMOUNT OF DEPOSIT	AMOUNT OF WITHDRAWAL	BALANCE
							1302. 96
7 20	146	The Dress Depot				135.22	135. 22
							1167.74
							5. 71
7 21	147	The Food Fest				40.79	-40. 79
	?	? ? ? ? TELEPHONE BILL?					03
	?				400.00		
7 28	150	Shoe Shack				73.60	
	?						
	152	The Book Bin				?	
8 2	153	?				approx. $20.00	

No one will get upset if you don't balance your checkbook.

You don't have to fight over who gets the crossword puzzle.

When it comes to the telephone, you have carte blanche. You can talk for hours without anyone humming and looking at his watch. And you won't have to fend off icy stares. On the other hand, if you want to chill out, sip wine and act like a vegetable, you can leave the phone off the hook and no one will ask you why.

Best of all, you never have to whisper when an old flame calls. And when you rewind the tape on your answering machine, all the messages will be for you!

You never have to whisper when an old flame calls.

You can flirt with everyone at a party.

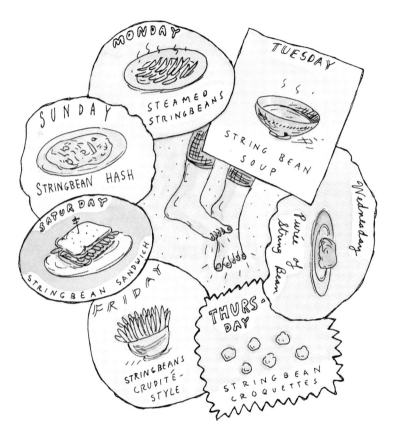

You can spend your last $50 on a pedicure, then eat string beans for dinner the rest of the week.

You can rearrange the furniture in your apartment in the middle of the night.

You can set all the clocks fast.

You can wear low-cut dresses without anyone raising an eyebrow.

Your mother can spend the weekend, no questions asked.

You can
decide on
Friday
afternoon to
go away for
the weekend.

You can watch *Star Trek* reruns all night on TV.

You know where all the pens and scratch paper are.

No one will open your mail by mistake.

Friends can drop
in at your
apartment anytime
they want.

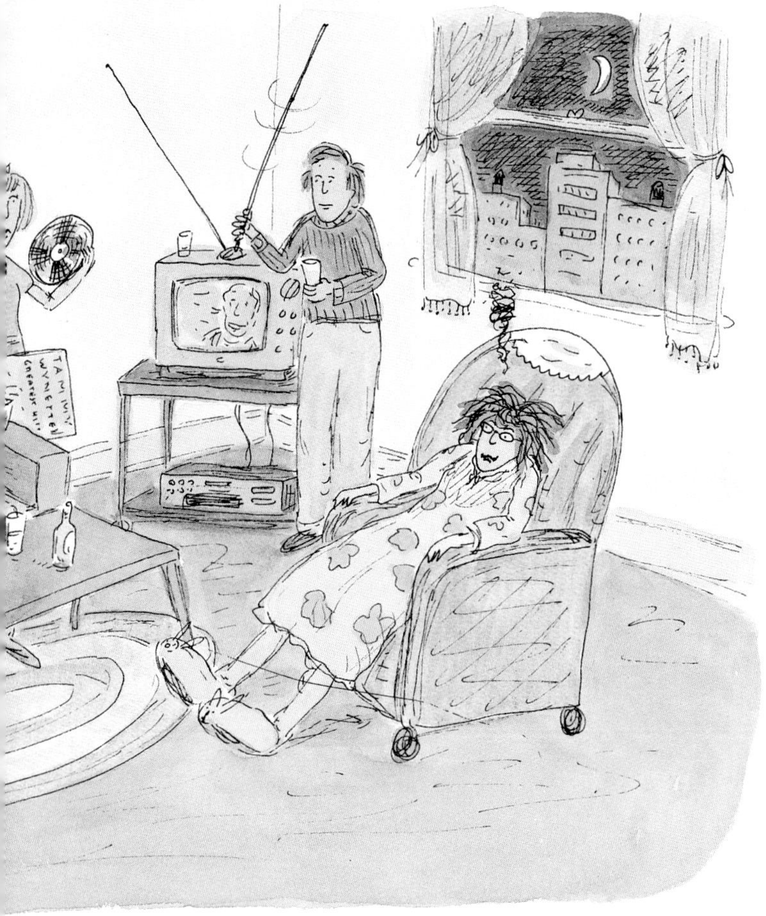
TAMMY WYNETTE
GREATEST HITS

You can switch
TV channels
without asking
anyone.

No one will criticize your painting, writing,
or cooking.

You can cry at old movies.

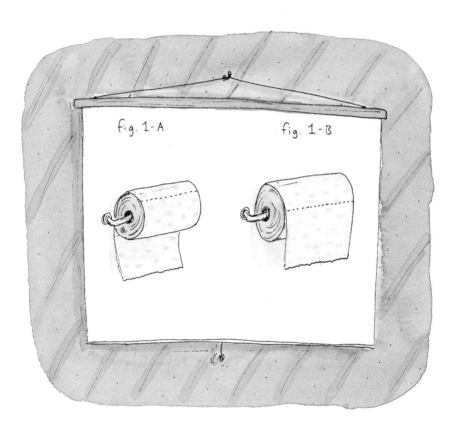

It doesn't matter which way the toilet tissue goes on the roll.

You never have to pretend you're not married.

Cute book?
your book
Could be better!

ABOUT THE AUTHOR *Could be you.*

ALLIA ZOBEL is a free-lance writer whose work has appeared in the New York *Times*, the Washington *Post*, *New Woman* magazine, and dozens of other newspapers and magazines. This is her first book.

ABOUT THE ILLUSTRATOR *Could be you.*

ROZ CHAST is the author of the recent *Proof of Life on Earth* and five other books of cartoons. She is a regular contributor to *The New Yorker* magazine.